Quick Lessons in Licensing

Licensing and Buying
Azure Reserved Instances and Server Subscriptions

By Louise Ulrick

Published by Licensing School.

Copyright © 2018 Licensing School.

All rights reserved.

ISBN: 978-1-911530-04-6.

No part of this publication may be reproduced or transmitted in any form or by any means, electronic or mechanical, without permission in writing from Licensing School.

First Edition – November 2018.

Table of Contents

USING THIS BOOK 1

BUYING AZURE CONSUMPTION SERVICES 2
   Payment in Arrears: Monthly Payments 2
   Upfront Payment: Monetary Commitment 4

UNDERSTANDING SUBSCRIPTIONS 5
   Enterprise Agreement 5
   Cloud Solution Provider Program 6

IMPORTANT PORTALS AND TOOLS 7
   Azure Management Portal 7
   Azure Enterprise Portal 7
   Partner Center Portal 8
   Azure Pricing Calculator 8

WINDOWS SERVER VIRTUAL MACHINES:
Using the All-Inclusive Consumption Based Virtual Machine 9

WINDOWS SERVER VIRTUAL MACHINES:
Using Existing Windows Server Licenses with Software Assurance 11
   Licensing with the Azure Hybrid Benefit 12
   Enabling the Azure Hybrid Benefit 14

WINDOWS SERVER VIRTUAL MACHINES:
Using an Azure Reserved Virtual Machine Instance 17
   Buying a Reserved Instance 18
   Paying for a Reserved Instance 19
   Assigning a Reserved Instance 19
   Changing a Reserved Instance 20

WINDOWS SERVER VIRTUAL MACHINES:
Using a Windows Server Subscription 25

© Licensing School 2018

WINDOWS SERVER VIRTUAL MACHINES:
Conclusions 29
   Summary of Options 29
   Final Notes on Pricing 30

SQL SERVER VIRTUAL MACHINES:
Using the All-Inclusive Consumption Based Virtual Machine 32

SQL SERVER VIRTUAL MACHINES:
Using Reserved Instances and the Azure Hybrid Benefit 34
   SQL Server Azure Hybrid Benefit 34
   Buying SQL Server Subscriptions 35
   Enabling the Azure Hybrid Benefit 35

KEEP UP TO DATE 38

ACKNOWLEDGEMENTS 38

© Licensing School 2018

USING THIS BOOK

This short book, which is part of our Quick Lessons in Licensing series, is a great introduction to the different ways of licensing Windows Server and SQL Server virtual machines in Azure. If you're new to this topic then you should read the book from start to finish to get an overview of this interesting subject. Equally, if you've attended one of our training courses then it's a useful resource to refer to after the course.

Originally, Microsoft offered virtual machines in Azure on a consumption basis, and then in February 2016 added the Azure Hybrid Benefit which made bringing your own licenses with Software Assurance a reality and helped to reduce overall costs. More recently they've added options such as Reservations and Server Subscriptions to open up the possible licensing options for customers even more.

This book gives you detailed information on all of these options and starts with an overview of how the Azure consumption services are paid for by different customers, and what portals they use to manage the services. We've focused on two ways of buying the services: through an Enterprise Agreement and through the Cloud Solution Provider (CSP) program. Typically, you would expect a larger customer to have historically bought all their licenses and Azure services through an Enterprise Agreement, and for smaller customers to have used a whole variety of different agreements. These days, CSP is becoming the main purchasing mechanism aimed at customers of all sizes, especially when they need partner services, since in CSP Microsoft only sells through partners rather than directly to customers.

Note that our intention is not to replace any of Microsoft's documentation; the purpose of the book is to teach you how Azure virtual machines are licensed, and where appropriate you should still refer to official contracts and other documents.

A final note: we all know that Microsoft's licensing changes at an astonishing pace – this book was produced in November 2018 and all information was accurate at the time of printing.

BUYING AZURE CONSUMPTION SERVICES

Today there are thousands of Azure services offering customers new ways to do what they're already doing in an on-premises infrastructure, or to extend their current solutions by using new and different services. The focus of this book is on Windows Server and SQL Server virtual machines, themselves Azure services.

Azure services are licensed and purchased in one of two ways. The first is when you pay a monthly fee for a certain amount of a particular service. Services licensed in this way are known as Plans and work, from a licensing and payment perspective, in a very similar way to Microsoft's Online Services. The second way is when you pay for the actual amount of services that are consumed, and it's these consumption services that we need to understand in relation to Azure virtual machines. We'll see that there are two ways that customers pay for these services: either with billing at the end of the month for the services they have used, or with an upfront payment for Azure services which is decremented as the services are consumed. In both cases you don't get a separate bill for each service, rather you get a single bill detailing all of the consumption services used.

The payment methods are not choices for a customer but rather depend on the program through which they're buying the Azure services. We'll look at the different options below.

Payment in Arrears: Monthly Payments

Server and Cloud Enrollment

We're going to start with the Server and Cloud Enrollment which is signed under an Enterprise Agreement. and requires a commitment to either SQL Server, the Core Infrastructure Server Suites, or the Visual Studio developer tools. The commitment is to have active Software Assurance for one of these components across the organization's entire installed base, having met some minimum requirements. Once that commitment is met, then the agreement can be used to purchase many other additional products, one of which is the

Azure services. The Server and Cloud Enrollment could also be signed with just Azure, but we'll come to that in the next section.

To see how the SCE works for Azure when it's not signed with Azure as the main component, let's take The Papaya Hire Company. This organization is signing an SCE for SQL Server and they've met all the requisite minimums for that product. While they're interested in Azure, they don't have any immediate plans to use it.

When an SCE is signed, Azure is automatically provisioned for the customer which means that they can use the Azure services as and when they are ready to, and there is no set up to be done in the Azure portals. So, The Papaya Hire Company sign their SCE and perhaps in the fourth month of their agreement start to use the Azure services. Payment is due for those services at the end of the month and invoices will continue to be issued at the end of each month for any services that have been consumed. However, there is no minimum amount of Azure services required to be consumed by The Papaya Hire Company and there is no ongoing commitment either.

Cloud Solution Provider Program

The other alternative for paying for the Azure consumption services at the end of a month is through the CSP program. To be completely precise I should mention that it's actually the partners who are billed by Microsoft at the end of the month for what their customers have used since Microsoft don't sell directly to customers through this program. Many partners charge their customers in this way too, but in fact they're not obliged to since Microsoft allows partners to present their own terms and conditions to customers.

Buying through a partner via CSP is often attractive to a customer who doesn't want to make any sort of commitment. In the SCE section above we saw that The Papaya Hire Company had to make a commitment to one of the SCE components before they could start using Azure on a consumption basis: in CSP there is no minimum requirement to get started and no ongoing commitment either.

Upfront Payment: Monetary Commitment

Let's get some more detail on the Enterprise Agreement now – an agreement under which an enrollment is signed. There are two enrollments available, and we've already looked at the Server and Cloud Enrollment which we saw requires a commitment to one of the server tools or, in fact, to the Azure consumption services. The second enrollment is the Enterprise Enrollment where a customer initially makes a commitment to cover all of their desktop devices with the Enterprise Products, or to a minimum of 500 Enterprise Online Services licenses, and is then eligible to start purchasing the Azure consumption services.

In both these enrollments a customer must make an upfront Monetary Commitment payment for the Azure consumption services. Each month this sum is decremented by the amount of consumption services actually used by the customer. There is a minimum monthly commitment per enrollment which is paid either once at the start of the three-year enrollment term (called Prepaid Monetary Commitment), or at the beginning of each year of the enrollment (called Annual Monetary Commitment). The minimums are $100 per month for an Enterprise Enrollment and $1,000 per month for the Server and Cloud Enrollment. This clearly translates into Annual Monetary Commitment minimums of $1,200 and $12,000, or Prepaid Monetary Commitment minimums of $3,600 and $36,000.

So, apart from the difference in the amounts, what's the difference between Annual and Prepaid Monetary Commitment? Well, it's all to do with what happens with unused funds at the end of a year. With Annual Monetary Commitment the funds must be used each year – there is no rollover of funds to a future year, whereas with Prepaid Monetary Commitment the funds are available for the full three years of the term and there's no requirement to use the funds in any particular year.

Now we know what happens with funds that haven't been used between years you may next be wondering what happens when a customer overspends on their Azure services – when they run out of Monetary Commitment. They may place a new Monetary Commitment order (of either type) at any time, or they may simply start making overage payments. And all that means is that they start paying at the end of the month for the services that they have used. So, there's a requirement to make some Monetary Commitment payment but that could be quite minimal if a customer prefers to pay for what they've used at the end of each month after the original Monetary Commitment amount is exhausted.

UNDERSTANDING SUBSCRIPTIONS

Subscriptions are an important element of buying Azure services. If you've attended one of my training courses, you'll know that I like to say this word with a capital "S" to emphasize that we're talking about something special. An Azure Subscription is like a container to which Azure services are assigned and it's the first thing that must be set up before customers can start to use Azure services. Where these Subscriptions are set up determines how the customer pays for the services, and they work slightly differently in the Enterprise Agreement and the Cloud Solution Provider program which are our two main focuses for this book.

Enterprise Agreement

For the Enterprise Agreement, when a non-Azure-only SCE is signed or when a Monetary Commitment order is processed, an Azure Enrollment is set up. Many customers will already have Azure Accounts where they have been perhaps trialing the Azure services by buying them through the direct portal, and these existing Accounts can be associated with an Enrollment so that future billing goes against the Volume Licensing agreement. It's within an Azure Account that Subscriptions are set up and every time an Azure service is provisioned the user chooses which Subscription the billing for that service should be recorded against.

An extra facility within the Azure Enterprise Portal means that a Department level can also be added and an Account can be associated with a Department if required. This means that an organization can see how they are using the

Azure services from an Enrollment perspective, or by Department, Account or Subscription.

You'll see this shown in the diagram below which represents the Enrollment for Periwinkle Packaging Solutions. Perhaps Account A is an existing one that they associated with their Enrollment and Accounts B and C ones that they created after the Enrollment was set up with the intention of being able to segment the spending on Azure Services:

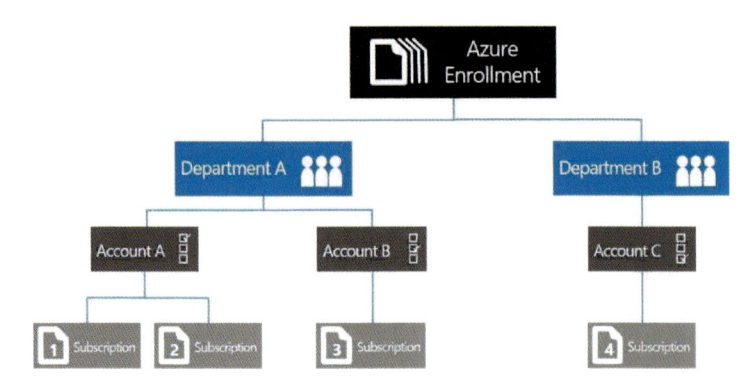

Figure 1: Enrollments, Departments, Accounts and Subscriptions

Cloud Solution Provider Program

In CSP there is no notion of Accounts, Departments, or Enrollments, there are just Subscriptions available. To set up a customer to start using the Azure consumption services in CSP, a partner just needs to create a single Subscription in the Partner Center portal. Additional Subscriptions may be set up to represent different projects or departments within the customer, as required.

IMPORTANT PORTALS AND TOOLS

All organizations which buy Azure services need to perform two key tasks: they need to set up the services from a technical perspective (provision virtual machines, for example) and they need to monitor their usage and spend of the services. There are a number of different portals that allow customers to do these things, and of course, since CSP is a partner-led program these tasks are often performed by the partner on behalf of the customer.

Azure Management Portal

The Azure Management portal (htttps://portal.azure.com) is where a technical person goes to provision the required resources and to assign them to a relevant Subscription. Within an Enterprise Agreement it's the customer who has access to this portal, but they may grant access to a partner for assistance if required. Within CSP, it's the partner who has default access to this portal on behalf of the customer, since the program is designed to enable partners to offer managed services to their customers.

Azure Enterprise Portal

The Azure Enterprise portal (https://ea.azure.com) is the portal that EA customers have access to. This portal gives usage information of each of the Azure services and both customers and their partners can see the amount of these services that have been consumed. There are a variety of reports and views in the portal and users can choose to see information at the Enrollment, Department, Account or Subscription level.

What's probably more important than the usage of the services, is the amount that is being spent on the services, and pricing information is automatically available in the Azure Enterprise portal for direct EA or SCE agreements. It is also available for indirect agreements, as long as the transacting partner has provided pricing information via the Markup facility in the portal. Obviously, it's in everyone's interests to make sure that this task has been performed – neither customers nor partners want a surprise bill with thousands of dollars of Azure services!

© Licensing School 2018

Partner Center Portal

The Partner Center portal (http://partnercenter.microsoft.com) is the Microsoft-provided portal for a CSP partner giving access to all of the tasks they need to carry out with regards to managing customers, selling licenses for Online Services such as Microsoft 365, and creating Azure Subscriptions. They can also use this portal to see the consumption and estimated spend of their customers' Azure consumption services.

However, as described earlier, the partner still uses the Azure Management portal to create resources for their customers. The technical person in the partner would access this portal from directly within the Partner Center portal so that they can authenticate as themselves to the Azure Management portal but manage resources directly on behalf of the customer.

It's also worth noting that customers buying through CSP don't have a Microsoft-provided portal to view consumption and spend of the Azure services since this is information that should be provided by the partner. Some partners design their own portals to give their customers a view on this information, while others offer more of a managed service with perhaps fixed-price offerings that don't require a customer to closely monitor their spend on all the different consumption services.

Azure Pricing Calculator
(https://azure.microsoft.com/en-us/pricing/calculator/)

The last thing to mention before we get started on the detail of licensing Windows Server and SQL Server virtual machines is a tool called the Azure Pricing Calculator. This calculator is publicly available to everyone and is very useful for obtaining estimated monthly pricing on all of the different Azure services. We'll use it throughout this book to enable us to compare the prices of the different options for purchasing Azure virtual machines.

WINDOWS SERVER VIRTUAL MACHINES:
Using the All-Inclusive Consumption Based Virtual Machine

Let's start our journey into understanding how customers can license virtual machines in Azure with an organization called Tangerine Truckers. They have an on-premises server farm running Windows Server virtual machines, which they've licensed with traditional Windows Server licenses acquired through their Volume Licensing agreement. One day they run out of capacity in that on-premises server farm and this is the event that makes them think about extending their server farm to Azure.

At this stage, running a proof of concept project could well be attractive, and they decide to deploy all-inclusive Windows Server virtual machines in Azure. This means that they pay for a virtual machine on a consumption basis: while it's up and running they incur charges, but when it's stopped, they don't. Prices for individual virtual machines are given as hourly billing prices, but the actual charging is per minute.

When you think about a Windows Server virtual machine it's important to always have in mind that there are two components: the infrastructure part (also called the base compute) and the Windows Server part. When Tangerine Truckers buy an all-inclusive Windows Server virtual machine, they pay a single fee for both components.

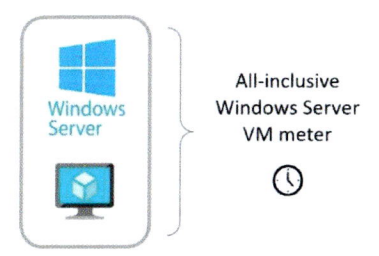

Figure 2: All-inclusive Windows Server Virtual Machine

As you would expect, if they choose a virtual machine with more resources (such as virtual cores or RAM) assigned to it, that will be more expensive than a virtual machine with less resources.

So, this is the first choice for paying for Windows Server virtual machines in Azure. It offers the highest level of flexibility – you just pay for what you need, but this comes at a price – it's the most expensive way of running virtual machines in Azure. The following sections consider other ways of paying for Windows Server virtual machines in Azure, all with considerable cost benefits over the all-inclusive virtual machine. To give us some sort of way of doing a comparison, let's use the Azure Pricing Calculator to get an estimate for the price of a particular virtual machine when it's been acquired in a particular way.

I'm going to be very consistent throughout and will always choose a D4 v2 virtual machine in the West US data center. You can see that the estimated monthly price for this virtual machine is $735.84.

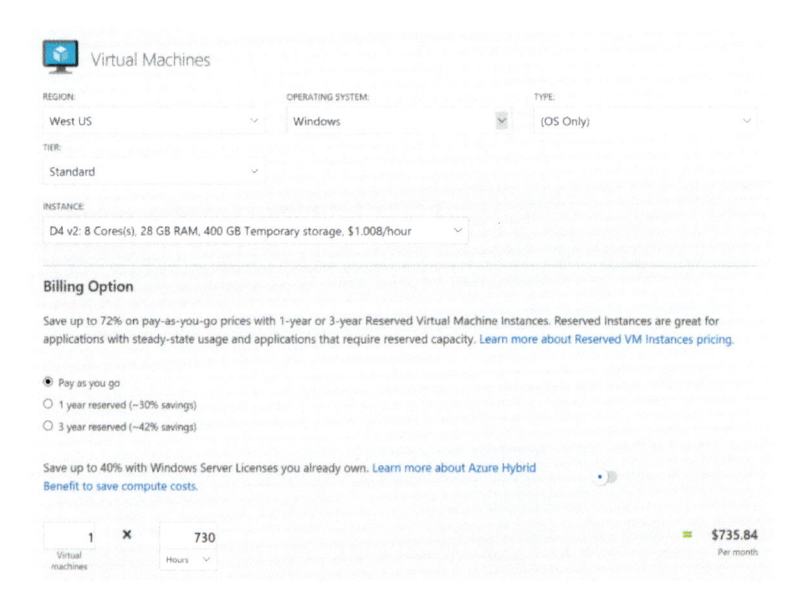

Figure 3: Azure Pricing Calculator - All-Inclusive Windows Server VM

Note that a virtual machine is also called an "instance"; I'll use this term occasionally in the following sections.

WINDOWS SERVER VIRTUAL MACHINES:
Using Existing Windows Server Licenses with Software Assurance

In this section we'll consider another customer, Goldfinger Food, who also have an on-premises server farm running Windows Server virtual machines. They too have licensed that with traditional Windows Server licenses acquired through their Volume Licensing agreement, and they've invested in Software Assurance for those licenses too.

So, what happened to Goldfinger Food such that they considered extending their server farm to Azure? Well, one of the physical servers in their server farm has come to the end of its life. At this point they have some choices: do they replace the hardware, with the inevitable delays in getting the purchase approved and the new server set up, or do they just start using some virtual machines in Azure? (Clearly in the real world it's not that simple, but let's go with it to learn about the licensing!)

James, the IT manager at Goldfinger Food, is good friends with the IT manager at Tangerine Truckers, Zak Suma, and they meet to talk about Zak's experiences in using virtual machines in Azure. Zak explains all about the all-inclusive virtual machines he's been using, paying a single fee for both the base compute and Windows Server components. James doesn't really think that solution is for him – if he retires a physical server he will have a number of unassigned Windows Server licenses that he won't be able to use, and he will end up paying for Windows Server again in the Azure virtual machine. Luckily for James, there's an alternative way for him to purchase his Windows Server virtual machines in Azure.

And so we come to the second way to license an Azure Windows Server virtual machine: to just pay for the compute power of the virtual machine on a consumption basis, and then to bring your own Windows Server licenses. When you pay for just the compute power of a virtual machine you actually buy a Linux Ubuntu virtual machine since there is no charge for this operating system;, this is often referred to as a base instance. You need active Software Assurance on the Windows Server licenses which gives access to the Azure Hybrid Benefit – the right to use those licenses either in an on-premises data center, or in Azure. This is how our diagram looks for this licensing option:

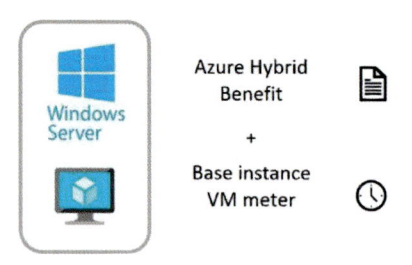

Figure 4: Windows Server VM – Using the Azure Hybrid Benefit

Licensing with the Azure Hybrid Benefit

Goldfinger Food do have active SA on their Windows Server licenses, so let's see how the Azure Hybrid Benefit works. Windows Server 2019 (and 2016 before that) is licensed with Core licenses which, in an on-premises solution, are assigned to a physical server based on the number of physical cores in that server. You need to assign a minimum of eight licenses to each processor, and this is a good number to remember for Azure virtual machines too, since the licenses must be kept together in groups of eight as you license the virtual machines.

Let's take some examples and license the following virtual machines in the Dv2 series family:

Instance	Cores
D1 v2	1
D2 v2	2
D3 v2	4
D4 v2	8
D5 v2	16

Figure 5: D1-5 v2 Virtual Machines

We'll start with the D4 v2 virtual machine which you can see has eight cores. We know the Windows Server Core licenses have to be kept together in groups of eight, so it seems straightforward to assign eight Windows Server Core licenses to this virtual machine – and this is indeed correct. Turning to the D5 v2 virtual machine with 16 cores and following the same rules, we'd need to assign 16 Core licenses to this virtual machine – or two groups of eight licenses. It's when you get to the lower-spec virtual machines that there's a temptation to forget the rules – you don't assign four Core licenses to the D3 v2 virtual machine, you must still assign eight Core licenses to it, and indeed to all the remaining virtual machines in the table.

There is just one more thing to consider in this section, and it's the difference in rights between a Windows Server 2019 Standard Core license and a Windows Server 2019 Datacenter Core license. With a Standard Core license, the Azure Hybrid Benefit rights are alternative – an organization can choose to use licenses in an on-premises data center following the usual on-premises licensing rules, or use them for Azure virtual machines following the "groups of eight" rule. I think this is how you would expect this benefit to work, so this hopefully feels straightforward.

The rules are different for Datacenter Core licenses though because the Azure Hybrid Use Benefit rights are additive. This means that you can use the licenses in an on-premises data center AND for Azure virtual machines. Take a look at the diagram in Figure 6: the on-premises servers (bottom left) are licensed correctly with 32 Core licenses each, for a total of eight groups of eight licenses. These licenses remain assigned to the servers, but they can also be used to license some base instance virtual machines in Azure. The number of cores of each virtual machine are shown in the circles – do you agree that Goldfinger Food has enough licenses for this configuration of Azure virtual machines? If you count the groups of eight licenses needed for each of the Azure virtual machines (1, 2-3-4-5, 6, 7, 8) then you should find that this is a completely compliant scenario.

Figure 6: Windows Server Azure Hybrid Benefit

Enabling the Azure Hybrid Benefit

So, how do you assign Windows Server licenses with SA to Azure Windows Server virtual machines? It's clearly an important task since you want to run a Windows Server virtual machine in Azure but want to issue the very clear instruction that you don't want to be charged for the Windows Server element since you are bringing your own licenses.

Let's start by looking at the process when you create a brand-new Windows Server virtual machine using a Gallery image in the Azure Management portal. Right at the bottom of the Basics tab is a "SAVE MONEY" section where you can specify that you already have appropriate Windows Server licenses as shown below:

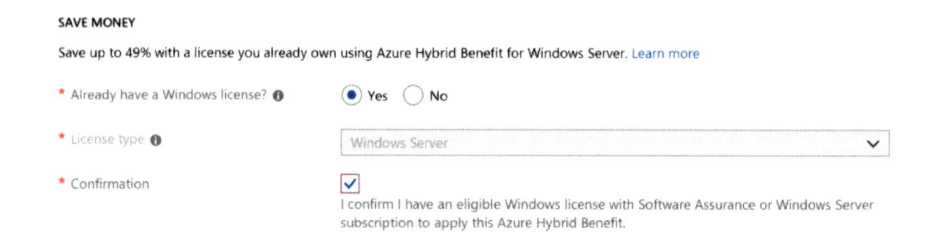

Figure 7: Confirming use of the Azure Hybrid Benefit

Checking this box will ensure that you can continue with the process of creating a Windows Server virtual machine but that you won't be charged for the Windows Server component because you've confirmed that you have enough licenses for the virtual machine being created.

So how does this work if you have a virtual machine that's already been created and you want to assign some Windows Server licenses to it and thus not be charged for the Windows Server component of that virtual machine?

Within the Azure Management portal you can view a list of all your virtual machines and add a column which shows whether or not the Azure Hybrid Benefit is enabled, as shown below:

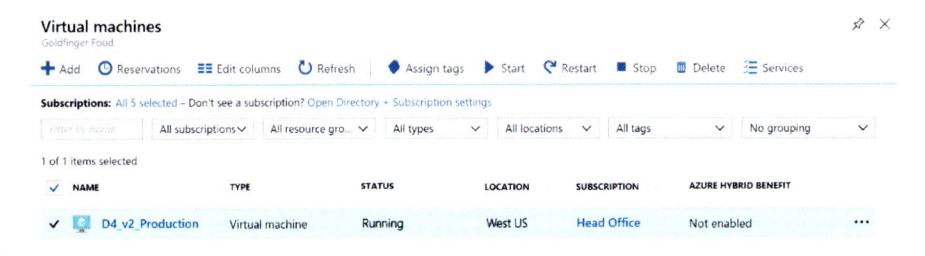

Figure 8: Checking Azure Hybrid Benefit Enablement

Here you can see that the single virtual machine that Goldfinger Food have running does not have the Azure Hybrid Benefit enabled and thus they will currently be being charged for the Windows Server component of that virtual machine. It's a simple matter of going to the Configuration settings of the virtual machine and then enabling the Azure Hybrid Benefit:

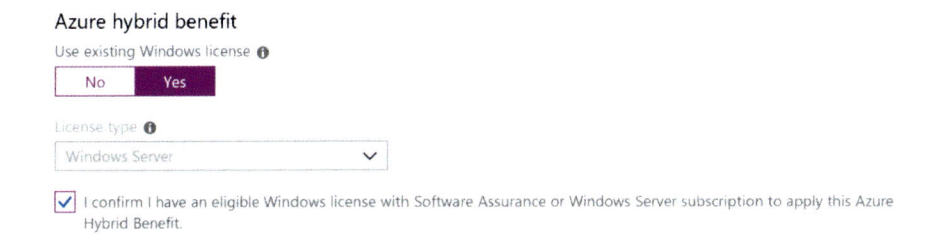

Figure 9: Enabling the Azure Hybrid Benefit for an Existing Virtual Machine

This will immediately change the way that the virtual machine is charged with no ongoing charges for the Windows Server component of the virtual machine.

So, this is the second way of paying for Windows Server virtual machines in Azure: paying for the base compute on a consumption basis, and then bringing your own licenses with Software Assurance to license the Windows Server component. Let's now return to the Azure Pricing Calculator to see the impact on the price:

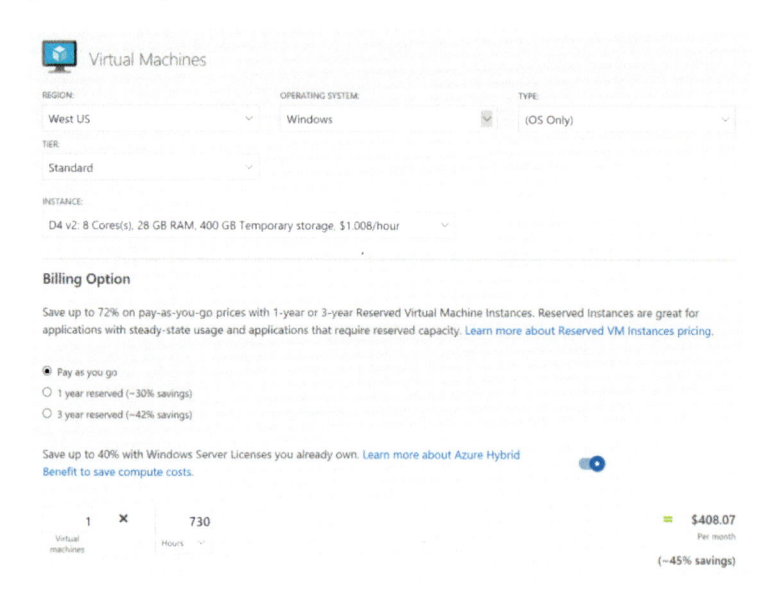

Figure 10: Azure Pricing Calculator – Using the Azure Hybrid Benefit

Again, for consistency, I've chosen the D4 v2 virtual machine in the West US data center, but this time I've activated the Azure Hybrid Benefit option. Note that what this does is to completely remove any charges for Windows Server for the virtual machine – it assumes you already have those licenses so doesn't include it in the costs here. However, I want to give you a realistic comparison between the options so let's take an estimate for SA pricing for 8 Core licenses per month to be $10.13, which gives us a total for this virtual machine of $418.20.

WINDOWS SERVER VIRTUAL MACHINES:
Using an Azure Reserved Virtual Machine Instance

In the previous section, James at Goldfinger Food was delighted that he can continue to use these Windows Server licenses that he's paid for. However, he's actually moving existing workloads to Azure and he realizes that he's paying the same prices for the base compute as someone who is running a virtual machine just for an hour or two. He's interested in a licensing solution that cuts his costs for the base compute part of the virtual machine too, so let's consider that now.

We need to turn our attention to Reservations and one particular member of the Reservations family, Reserved Virtual Machine Instances. Microsoft launched these in November 2017, and you'll be glad to hear that we're going to use their abbreviated name, Reserved Instances, from now on!

So, what is a Reserved Instance and how will it help Goldfinger Food in their quest for the most cost-effective way to license a Windows Server virtual machine in Azure? Well, a Reserved Instance is a way of getting the best possible pricing for the base compute part of a virtual machine by paying upfront for a one or a three-year term. This means that to license the two parts of a Windows Server virtual machine in Azure, Goldfinger Food will use a Reserved Instance to pay for the base compute part, and their existing Windows Server licenses with SA to license the Windows Server part.

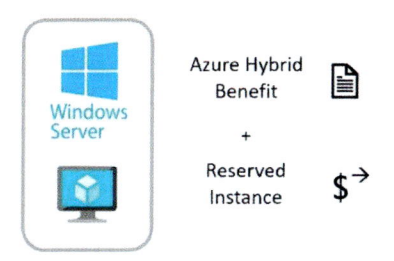

Figure 11: Windows Server VM – Reserved Instance + Azure Hybrid Benefit

Buying a Reserved Instance

Reserved Instances are available through both the Enterprise Agreement and CSP, and although a partner can transact them through the Partner Center portal, I think it's easiest to use the Azure Management portal, which is also the portal an EA customer would use. After you've selected the Reservations category and chosen to create a new Reserved Instance, this is the form that needs to be completed:

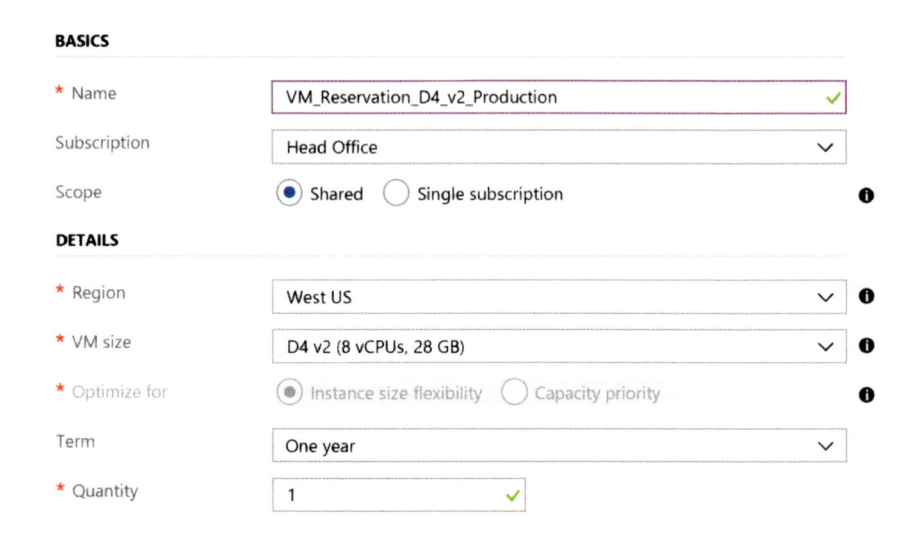

BASICS	
* Name	VM_Reservation_D4_v2_Production ✓
Subscription	Head Office
Scope	● Shared ○ Single subscription

DETAILS	
* Region	West US
* VM size	D4 v2 (8 vCPUs, 28 GB)
* Optimize for	● Instance size flexibility ○ Capacity priority
Term	One year
* Quantity	1 ✓

Figure 12: Buying a Reserved Instance

You can customize the name of the Reservation, otherwise it will automatically generate a name composed of the date and time the Reservation was ordered. Next you need to make a decision about Subscriptions. We saw earlier that a Subscription is important within the Azure world since every resource that is created needs to be assigned to a Subscription. Here you choose whether a Reserved Instance should be assigned to a single Subscription or shared amongst all Subscriptions. You can see that Goldfinger Food have chosen the Shared option and we'll see the impact of that choice in the "Assigning a Reserved Instance" section below.

Then you need to commit to the data center (West US) and virtual machine (D4 v2) that you want to pre-pay for the base compute. You can see that the next options for "Optimize for" are greyed out – this is because we've chosen "Shared" as the "Scope" option at the top. For most customers, having instance size flexibility is going to be attractive (which is what is chosen by default) rather than needing capacity priority which reserves data center capacity for the exact type of virtual machine chosen. Again, we'll look at Instance Flexibility in detail in a section below.

Then the last choices are to decide on a one or three-year commitment with, of course, the greatest savings to be achieved with a three-year commitment, and finally the number of virtual machines for which you want to pre-pay for the base compute. As you can see, Goldfinger Food are starting small with just the one!

Paying for a Reserved Instance

We've seen how Reserved Instances are ordered through the Azure Management portal, let's now look at how they're paid for. If Goldfinger Food were buying through a CSP partner, then the partner would carry out the steps in the previous section and they would be charged upfront for the chosen term. They are likely to charge Goldfinger Food in the same way but, as I mentioned in a previous section, actually the partner may compile any payment terms that are acceptable to, or desired by, Goldfinger Food.

If, on the other hand, Goldfinger Food have an Enterprise Agreement, then they may well complete the purchase themselves – they are able to give a partner access to carry out tasks like this if they want to. Either way, the upfront payment for the Reserved Instance is taken from their existing Monetary Commitment balance or, if that is at zero, as an overage payment on their next monthly bill.

Assigning a Reserved Instance

Goldfinger Food have successfully purchased a Reserved Instance so how do they now assign it to a virtual machine? Actually, there's nothing for them to do at all. If there is already a virtual machine running which matches both the type of virtual machine in the Reservation (D4 v2) and the region (West US), then the Reserved Instance is automatically applied to the virtual machine. This will immediately change the way the virtual machine is charged, removing any costs for the base compute component.

If they create a new virtual machine using a Gallery image in the Azure Management portal, then the existing Reservation will automatically be applied to that virtual machine as long as, again, it matches the type of virtual machine and the region.

One question I'm always asked at this point in a course is what happens when the Reserved Instance comes to the end of its term. There will be notifications sent out when the Reserved Instance approaches the end of its one or three-year term, but if a new Reservation is not purchased, all that happens is that the billing for the base compute of the virtual machine reverts to a consumption basis.

There's one more element we need to consider in this section and it's the scope choices that were made when the Reservation was purchased. A Reservation can be assigned to a single Subscription or to all Subscriptions and this is taken into account when the automatic matching just described takes place. If a single Subscription has been chosen, then the system only looks within that single Subscription for a match to apply the Reservation to, whereas if all Subscriptions are chosen then it looks across all of them.

Changing a Reserved Instance

Customers get a good price for Reserved Instances because they have paid upfront and have made some choices in terms of virtual machine size and Azure data center, which means that Microsoft can do some capacity planning. However, things may change for a business over time, especially if they've committed to a three-year Reserved Instance. So, let's now take a look as to what flexibility there is post-purchase.

Scope

As you know, the scope determines whether the Reserved Instance is assigned to a single Subscription or to all Subscriptions, and this can easily be changed at any time. It's just a case of going to the Configuration settings of the Reservation in the Azure Management portal and choosing the new option required.

Instance Flexibility

Instance flexibility is something that was introduced after the launch of Reserved Instances and means that a Reservation isn't tied to an exact virtual machine type any more, but rather to a family of virtual machines. This means that if a business' requirements for their virtual machines changes within a family, the Reserved Instance is still applied automatically to different virtual machines.

As usual, let's look at an example to understand this in a bit more detail. A few pages ago, Goldfinger Food bought a Reserved Instance for a D4 v2 virtual machine in the West US data center. Now, although they chose a D4 v2 virtual machine, they've actually purchased units of base compute in the Dv2 series family for the West US data center according to the ratios shown in the following table:

Instance	Ratio
D1 v2	1
D2 v2	2
D3 v2	4
D4 v2	8
D5 v2	16

Figure 13: Dv2 Family Ratios

You can see that they purchased eight units and if they run a D4 v2 virtual machine then that Reserved Instance will be applied to that virtual machine and cover the base compute costs in their entirety. But Goldfinger Food could now change their mind and decide to run two D3 v2 virtual machines instead of the original D4 v2. If we calculate the units of base compute required, we see that it would again total eight units and the Reserved Instance would again cover the base compute costs in their entirety. So finally, what happens if they want to use a D5 v2 virtual machine which is 16 units? Well, the Reserved Instance will cover half of the base compute costs and the remainder will be charged on a consumption basis on the relevant base compute meter.

Exchange

Instance Flexibility is great when Goldfinger Food want to change the virtual machine type within a family and within the same data center, but clearly there will be occasions when this isn't enough flexibility. So, for situations outside those covered by Instance Flexibility, there's the possibility of exchanging a Reserved Instance which allows you to change both the virtual machine family and the Azure data center if you need to.

What happens here is that at the point of the required change, credit is calculated for the remaining term of the Reserved Instance and that can be applied against a completely new one or three-year Reserved Instance. This can be for any virtual machine type in any data center, the only rule being that the value of the new Reserved Instance must be higher than the credit amount. Goldfinger Food would pay for the exchanged Reserved Instance in exactly the same way as if it was a brand new one.

The actual process is carried out in the Azure Management portal – by the customer or their partner dependent on the program – by simply viewing the Reservation and choosing the Exchange button.

Cancel

But what happens if Goldfinger Food's needs change so much that they no longer need any sort of Reserved Instance? Well, a Reservation can be cancelled, if required. This again is carried out from the Azure Management portal, by choosing the Refund button.

Credit is again calculated for the remaining term and an early termination fee of 12% is deducted, and then the balance is refunded. If the original Reserved Instance had been purchased through an Enterprise Agreement, it is refunded to the original mechanism used to purchase it. If Monetary Commitment was used, it is returned to the available balance, and if overage was used then it shows as a credit on the monthly overage invoice. If the Reserved Instance was purchased through CSP then it is the partner's account that is refunded, and they credit their customer according to their own agreed terms and conditions.

Note that Reserved Instances that have not been used may be cancelled with no fee within 48 hours, but if refunds are processed then they are capped at $50,000 per customer per calendar year.

Transfer

And finally, let's consider some questions that I'm frequently asked on training courses:

- Can a Reserved Instance be transferred between customers?
- If a customer transitions between programs such as between EA and CSP, can the Reserved Instances be transferred as well?
- If a customer transitions from one CSP partner to another, are the Reserved Instances transferred as well?

And the answer to all of these questions? No – Reserved Instances can't be transferred in any of these ways.

So, that's the third way of paying for Windows Server virtual machines in Azure: paying upfront for the base compute using a Reserved Instance, and then bringing your own licenses with Software Assurance to license the Windows Server component. Let's return to the Azure Pricing Calculator again to see what the impact on price is:

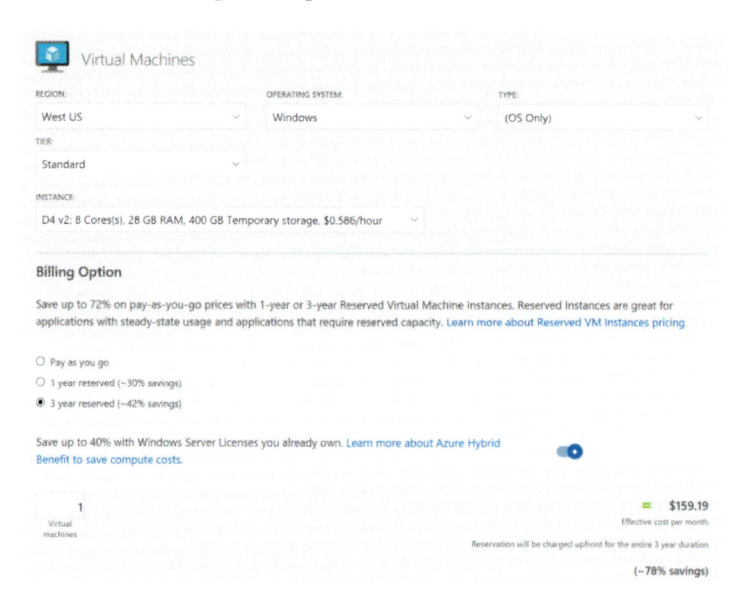

Figure 14: Azure Pricing Calculator – Reserved Instance + Azure Hybrid Benefit

I've chosen the usual virtual machine in the usual data center and I've kept the Azure Hybrid Benefit option selected. However, this time I've also selected the "3 year reserved" option which, as you can see, has decreased the price significantly. Again, we need to add some costs for SA since they're not included here – let's take the $10.13 that we used before – and that gives a total for this solution of $169.32.

WINDOWS SERVER VIRTUAL MACHINES:
Using a Windows Server Subscription

Continuing our journey through all of the different options, let's now return to our first customer – Tangerine Truckers. They had decided to extend their server farm to Azure, and the last time we spoke to them they were happy with the notion of the all-inclusive Windows Server virtual machine. However, time has now moved on, and they're no longer in the proof of concept stage for their virtual machines, and they're starting to want to get the best possible pricing as they run full-time workloads in Azure.

So, Zak the IT Manager met with his good friend James from Goldfinger Food to see how they're paying for their Windows Server virtual machines. Zak was (of course) extremely interested to hear about Reserved Instances as the best way of paying for the base compute part of the virtual machine. However, he was disappointed to learn that the best way of licensing the Windows Server component was to bring his own licenses via the Azure Hybrid Benefit. Tangerine Truckers haven't had a policy of buying Software Assurance on their Windows Server licenses, so he can't make use of this.

However, there are two further options that will be of interest to Zak so let's take a look at those now. Let's assume he took James' advice and purchased a Reserved Instance. We know that the Reserved Instance will be applied automatically to a running virtual machine and he won't be charged for base compute, but how will he now be charged for the Windows Server component? Well, there's a Windows Server core meter and that will be applied automatically to the virtual machine so that he'll pay for Windows Server on a consumption basis.

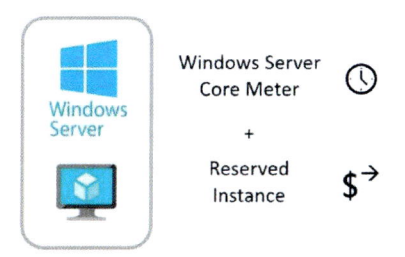

Figure 15: Windows Server VM – Reserved Instance + Core Meter

As usual, let's take a look at the Azure Pricing Calculator to see what options you'd choose and to find out what sort of prices Zak will pay for this option:

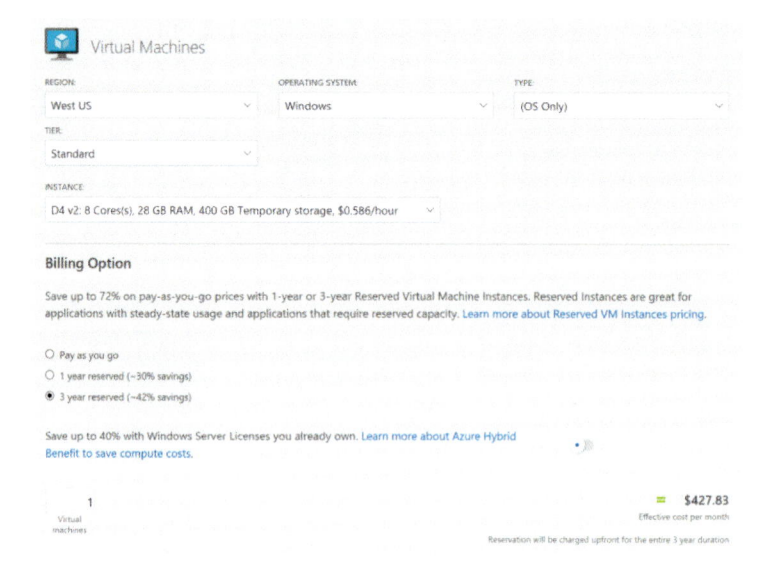

Figure 16: Azure Pricing Calculator - Reserved Instance + Core Meter

In terms of options, this time I've selected the "3 year reserved" option again and deselected the Azure Hybrid Benefit. You can see that the estimated price is $427.83 – compared to $735.84 for the all-inclusive virtual machine he started out with.

So Zak will make considerable savings by purchasing a Reserved Instance for the base compute and this is a convenient, automatic solution. However, Zak is very aware that any Azure service that he pays for on a meter, while flexible, is not going to be the most cost-effective way of paying for something when he's prepared to make a commitment to the service. And this is where he's likely to be interested in the second option – buying a Server Subscription for Windows Server.

A Server Subscription for Windows Server is pretty much exactly what it sounds like – you're acquiring Windows Server licenses on a subscription basis. It's just Windows Server Standard licenses that are available, and you buy them in packs of eight Core licenses.

They include the Azure Hybrid Benefit and that means that you can choose to assign the licenses to an Azure base instance (which is what we're primarily interested in) or choose to use those licenses with an on-premises infrastructure. We looked at the rules for licensing Azure Windows Server virtual machines via the Azure Hybrid Benefit acquired through a Volume Licensing license with Software Assurance, and (thankfully) the rules here are exactly the same: you need to assign a minimum of eight licenses to a virtual machine and you need to keep the licenses together in groups of eight.

So, just to recap, check you're happy with the requirements in the following table:

Instance	Cores	Server Subscriptions Required
D1 v2	1	1 x 8-pack
D2 v2	2	1 x 8-pack
D3 v2	4	1 x 8-pack
D4 v2	8	1 x 8-pack
D5 v2	16	2 x 8-packs

Figure 17: Assigning Windows Server Subscriptions

So what are the rules for transacting them? They're quite a new offering, just being launched in July 2018, and are currently only available through CSP, where the partner transacts them through the Partner Center portal. As far as the payment options go, this will sound familiar: they're available for a one or three-year term via a single upfront payment. Cancellations ARE allowed, but the terms are different to a Reserved Instance: you can cancel within 60 days for a full refund, but there are no pro-rated refunds available after that time.

In terms of how Windows Server Subscriptions are assigned to running and new virtual machines, they work in exactly the same way as the traditional Windows Server licenses which we looked at above. You simply need to check the Azure Hybrid Benefit box when you create a virtual machine and enable the Azure Hybrid Benefit on an existing virtual machine if you've got sufficient licenses you can assign to it.

So that leads us to our final diagram and we see that there are two ways for being eligible for the Azure Hybrid Benefit – via licenses with active SA or by buying a Server Subscription.

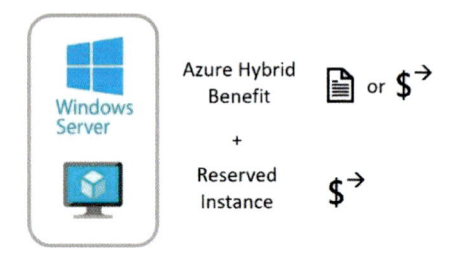

Figure 18: Windows Server VM – Reserved Instance + Azure Hybrid Benefit Options

In terms of pricing, we can't use the Azure Pricing Calculator since the options for Server Subscriptions only appear to CSP partners. Thus, we'll use an advertised Estimated Retail Price of $582 for a 3-year Server Subscription and divide by 36 to get a monthly figure of $16.17. Added to the price the calculator showed on page 24, which was $159.19 for the three-year Reserved Instance, gives a total of $175.36 for this particular solution.

WINDOWS SERVER VIRTUAL MACHINES: Conclusions

Summary of Options

We've considered a couple of customers and the options that might be appropriate for them as they consider their needs for Windows Server virtual machines in Azure. These are their choices in summary, with the prices attached. Where there are two prices it's because there are two ways of acquiring the Azure Hybrid Benefit – either through active SA on existing Windows Server licenses, or by buying Windows Server Subscriptions.

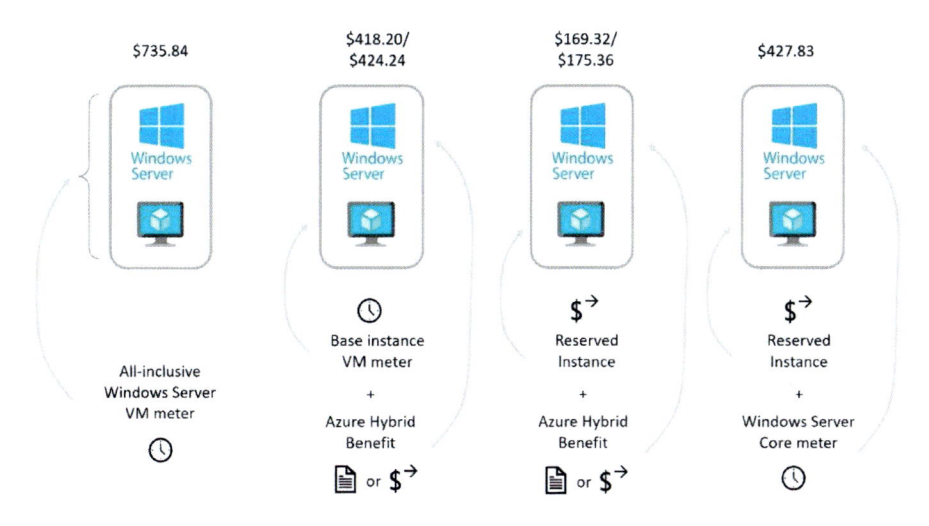

$735.84	$418.20/ $424.24	$169.32/ $175.36	$427.83
All-inclusive Windows Server VM meter	Base instance VM meter + Azure Hybrid Benefit	Reserved Instance + Azure Hybrid Benefit	Reserved Instance + Windows Server Core meter

Figure 19: Windows Server VMs – Summary of Options

In reality, would you consider all of these options as you made a choice as to how to license a Windows Server virtual machine in Azure? I think you would probably restrict yourself to two options in two different scenarios:

- In a proof of concept or other short-term project, then use the all-inclusive virtual machine since that gives you the maximum flexibility
- If you're running more consistent or full-time workloads then purchase a Reserved Instance for the base compute, and make use of the Azure Hybrid Benefit through active SA or Server Subscriptions

Final Notes on Pricing

I should emphasize that I've chosen 3-year Reserved Instances and Server Subscriptions when I've compared the pricing for the options throughout this section. We've compared monthly prices but remember that the payment terms for both of these offers is in full, upfront – we're just using monthly pricing as a comparison.

In the previous section I recommended the Reserved Instance + Azure Hybrid Benefit option for a consistent or full-time workload. But, you might be wondering, does it really have to be full-time or is there some leeway? There is – take a look at the chart below where I've used the slightly more expensive Reserved Instance + Server Subscriptions option:

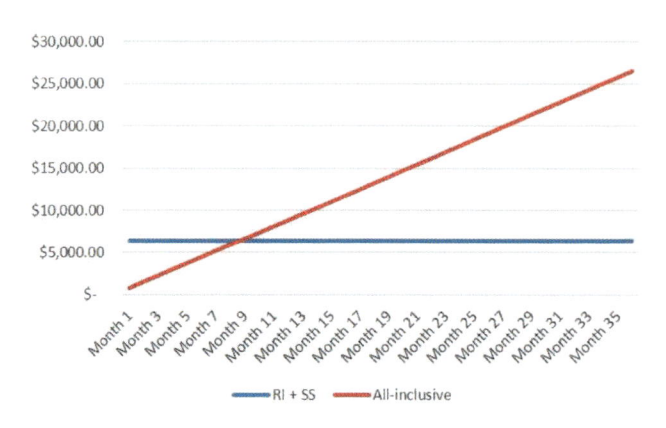

Figure 20: Windows Server VMs – Cost Comparison Chart

The blue line represents the amount that you pay upfront for the 3-year Reserved Instance and Server Subscriptions – a fixed fee of $6,312.96. The red line shows the total you will pay month by month if you use an all-inclusive virtual machine, and you can see that in month nine the total you've paid is now more than if you'd paid for the Reserved Instance and Server Subscription – and you're going to carry on paying more as you continue to use the virtual machine. If you use the virtual machine for the full 36 months, then the total all-inclusive bill will be $26,490.24.

This chart shows how "full-time" a workload needs to be – as long as I'm running it for about nine months out of the 36 then the Reserved Instance + Server Subscription is a cost-effective option.

In general, if you divide the cost of the Reserved Instance + Server Subscriptions by the total amount spent on an all-inclusive virtual machine it will give you an accurate break-even figure. Here it's $6,312.96 / $26,490.24 = 0.24. This means that as long as the workload runs for at least 24% of the time, then you will save money by paying upfront. Of course, that could be just 6 hours a day, or a week a month, or just 3 months in a year over the 36-month period.

SQL SERVER VIRTUAL MACHINES:
Using the All-Inclusive Consumption Based Virtual Machine

Our journey through the options for licensing a Windows Server virtual machine in Azure was thorough, but in summary we saw that there are two main options to consider – an all-inclusive virtual machine when flexibility is key, and a combination of Reserved Instances and bringing your own licenses when cost is the primary concern for a longer-term workload.

This is exactly the same for SQL Server and thus, in this section we can tackle the options for a SQL Server virtual machine much more quickly since we already know much of what we need to.

So, the first option is the all-inclusive virtual machine as shown below:

Figure 21: All-inclusive SQL Server Virtual Machine

This time there are three components in the virtual machine: the base compute, Windows Server, and SQL Server. The single fee covers costs for all three of these components.

Again, let's use the Azure Pricing Calculator to get an idea of what this solution might cost:

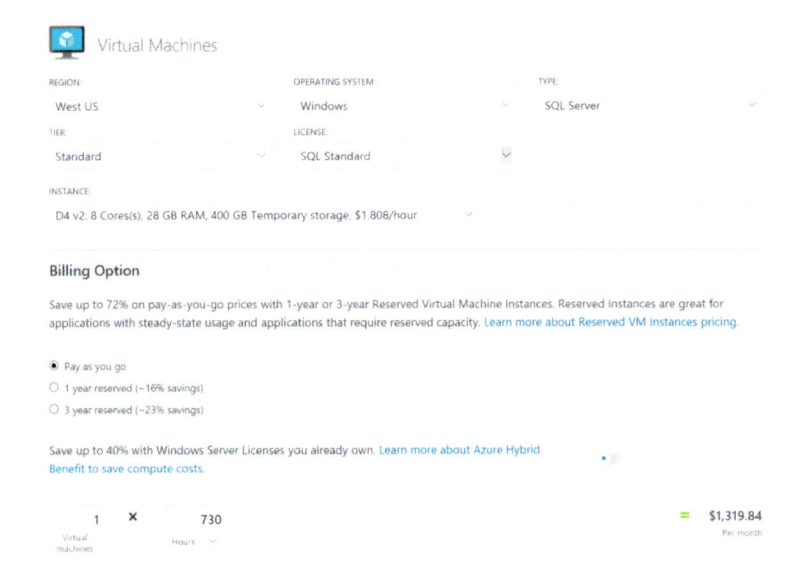

Figure 22: Azure Pricing Calculator - All-inclusive SQL Server VM

You can see I've again been consistent in the choices I've made – it's a D4 v2 virtual machine in the West US data center and all I've done differently is to select SQL Server as the "Type" and to choose "SQL Standard" as the "License". This gives us an estimated monthly cost of $1,319.84 for this solution.

SQL SERVER VIRTUAL MACHINES:
Using Reserved Instances and the Azure Hybrid Benefit

The other option we'll consider is where we split out the three components of the virtual machine and look for the most cost-effective ways of licensing each component. As we saw before, a Reserved Instance is the best way of paying for the base compute, and the Azure Hybrid Benefit is the best way of licensing both the Windows Server and SQL Server components. And, again, customers can do this if they have Software Assurance on existing licenses, or they can buy Server Subscriptions.

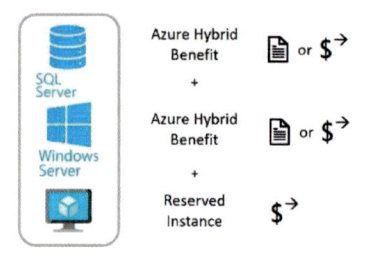

Figure 23: SQL Server VM – Reserved Instance + Azure Hybrid Benefit Options

SQL Server Azure Hybrid Benefit

There are no differences in buying either the Reserved Instances or the Server Subscriptions for Windows Server when you want to run SQL Server in a virtual machine, so we'll focus on the new things you need to know.

It's the Azure Hybrid Benefit that allows customers to choose where to use their licenses – either with an Azure virtual machine or in an on-premises infrastructure. Customers are eligible for the Azure Hybrid Benefit if they have active Software Assurance on existing SQL Server Standard or Enterprise Core licenses, or if they buy Server Subscriptions for SQL Server.

When you're assigning licenses to a SQL Server virtual machine you need to assign a Core license to cover each virtual core, with a minimum of four Core licenses assigned to a single virtual machine.

Again, check you're happy with these rules, making sure you agree with the following table:

Instance	Cores	Core Licenses Required
D1 v2	1	4
D2 v2	2	4
D3 v2	4	4
D4 v2	8	8
D5 v2	16	16

Figure 24: Table

These rules apply for both SQL Server Standard and Enterprise editions.

Buying SQL Server Subscriptions

SQL Server Subscriptions have much in common with Windows Server Subscriptions – they are only available through CSP and are thus transacted by the partner through Partner Center. The payment terms are the same too – they are available for a one or three-year term and must be paid for in full upfront, with cancellations only possible in the first 60 days. In terms of the editions, Core licenses for both Standard and Enterprise edition are available, and they are sold in 2-packs.

Enabling the Azure Hybrid Benefit

In the Windows Server section we saw that to stop charges for the Windows Server portion of a virtual machine you just needed to enable the Azure Hybrid Benefit whether you're creating a new virtual machine, or you have an existing virtual machine.

Things are a little bit different with a SQL Server virtual machine so let's take a look at that now. When you create a new SQL Server virtual machine there are no images in the Gallery that let you specify that you already have both Windows Server and SQL Server licenses and thus that you want to apply them to that virtual machine so that you don't get charged for those products. There is a Bring Your Own License (BYOL) image for a SQL Server virtual machine available for Enterprise Agreement customers but it doesn't (currently!) allow you to specify that you also have Windows Server licenses. So, the recommendation when you're creating a new SQL Server virtual machine from Gallery images is to actually create a new Windows Server machine and activate the Azure Hybrid Benefit for that, and then install SQL Server into that virtual machine. This means that you won't be charged for either Windows Server or SQL Server.

Alternatively, if you have an existing SQL Server virtual machine, you could deploy that to Azure, activate the Azure Hybrid Benefit for Windows Server, and again you won't be charged for either Windows Server or SQL Server.

Let's take our usual look at costs for this option, and here the Azure Pricing Calculator isn't particularly helpful. If you select the Azure Hybrid Benefit option, it just removes the Windows Server costs rather than both the Windows Server and SQL Server costs. Thus, we'll calculate the pricing manually.

Let's arm ourselves with some figures for the SQL Server portion. An appropriate estimate for Software Assurance for 8 Core licenses would be $310 per month, and a 3-year Server Subscription for SQL Server Standard is $4,254 for a 2-core pack and thus multiplying by 4 (for 8 cores) and dividing by 36 (to get a monthly price) gives us $472.67. I've put these figures into the table below, along with the figures we used before for the Windows Server and Reserved Instance components. As a reminder, the monthly cost of the all-inclusive SQL Server virtual machine is $1,319.84.

	Software Assurance estimate per month	Server Subscription per month
Windows Server	$10.13	$16.17
SQL Server	$310.00	$472.67

+

Reserved Instance	$159.19	$159.19
Total	**$479.32**	**$648.03**

To create the break-even chart below I used the Reserved Instance + Server Subscriptions total for 36 months giving a figure of $648.03 x 36 = $23,329.08 for the blue line. Then I increased the monthly figure by $1,319.84 each month to give the red line, and a 36 month total of $47,514.24.

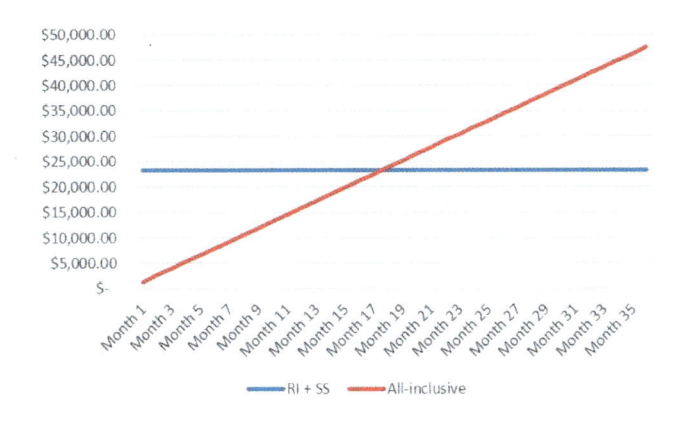

Figure 25: SQL Server VMs – Cost Comparison Chart

You can see that the break-even point occurs approximately in month 18. If we do the calculation (23,329.08 / 47,514.24) to find how "full-time" the workload needs to be, we have a figure of 0.49 or a shade under 50%. This means that if you have a SQL Server virtual machine running for 12 hours a day, or 2 weeks a month or for 18 out of the 36 months, then the Reserved Instance + Server Subscriptions option is a cost-effective choice.

KEEP UP TO DATE

We've got some great ways for you to keep up to date with Microsoft licensing:

- Subscribe to our blog and receive regular updates: www.licensingschool.co.uk/licensing-blog/
- Sign up for our free fortnightly licensing newsletter: www.licensingschool.co.uk/school-report/
- Keep in touch on social media – you'll find us on Twitter, LinkedIn and Facebook – just search for Licensing School

ACKNOWLEDGEMENTS

Thanks to Simon Taylor for proof reading with the beadiest eyes in the business; if there are still errors then the fault is mine as I had the final say. Thanks also to Simon for coming up with all the fictional company names that are used throughout.

Thanks to Simona Millham and Sally Finlayson, the creative brains behind the graphics used in this book. Again, if any are less than perfect it's due to my tweaking.

A special thank you to Paul Burgum, a business partner in a million, without whose guidance, support, and endless supply of good ideas I would not have been able to put this book and all our other resources together.

Louise Ulrick